HOW TO MAKE MONEY IN STOCKS

A Guide to Successful Stock Market Investing

MITT Creations

This Book Is Belongs To

....

....

....

....

....

Chapter 1

I: Introduction to Stock Market Investing

Welcome to **"How to Make Money in Stocks,"** where we embark on an enlightening journey into the world of stock market investing. In this introductory chapter, we lay the groundwork for understanding the basics of stock market investing, explore the benefits and risks associated with investing in stocks, and emphasize the importance of setting realistic expectations for returns and risk tolerance.

A. Understanding the Basics of Stock Market Investing

Stock market investing involves purchasing shares of ownership in publicly traded companies, with the aim of generating returns through dividends and capital appreciation. The stock market serves as a marketplace where buyers and sellers trade stocks, allowing investors to participate in the growth and profitability of companies across various industries and sectors. Understanding key concepts such as stocks, stock exchanges, market indices, and trading mechanisms is essential for navigating the complexities of the stock market with confidence and clarity.

B. Benefits and Risks of Investing in Stocks

Investing in stocks offers a multitude of benefits, including the potential for long-term wealth accumulation, portfolio diversification, and participation in economic growth. Stocks historically have outperformed other asset classes over the long term, providing investors with the opportunity to build wealth and achieve financial goals. However, it's crucial to recognize the inherent risks associated with stock market investing, including volatility, market fluctuations, and the potential for loss of capital. By balancing the benefits and risks of investing in stocks, investors can make informed decisions and mitigate potential downside while maximizing potential returns.

C. Setting Realistic Expectations for Returns and Risk Tolerance

One of the keys to successful stock market investing is setting realistic expectations for returns and understanding your risk tolerance. While stocks have the potential to generate significant returns over time, they also carry inherent risks that can result in short-term losses and fluctuations in portfolio value. It's essential for investors to assess their risk tolerance, financial goals, and investment time horizon before entering the stock market. By aligning investment decisions with personal objectives and risk preferences, investors can navigate market volatility with resilience and discipline, staying focused on long-term wealth accumulation rather than short-term fluctuations.

As we embark on this journey into the world of stock market investing, remember that knowledge is power. By understanding the basics of stock market investing, recognizing the benefits and risks, and setting realistic expectations, you lay the foundation for a successful and fulfilling investment journey. In the chapters that follow, we will delve deeper into the principles, strategies, and techniques for making informed investment decisions and achieving financial success in the stock market.

Chapter 2

II: Getting Started with Stock Market Investing

In this chapter, we dive into the essential steps to get started with stock market investing, from opening a brokerage account to understanding the different types of stocks and performing research and analysis before making investment decisions.

A. Opening a Brokerage Account

The first step in getting started with stock market investing is to open a brokerage account. A brokerage account serves as your gateway to the stock market, allowing you to buy and sell stocks, mutual funds, exchange-traded funds (ETFs), and other securities. When choosing a brokerage firm, consider factors such as fees, commissions, investment options, research tools, and customer service. Whether you opt for a traditional full-service brokerage or a discount online brokerage, ensure that the brokerage aligns with your investment goals and preferences.

B. Understanding Different Types of Stocks

Before diving into stock market investing, it's essential to understand the different types of stocks available in the market. The two primary types of stocks are common stocks and preferred stocks. Common stocks represent ownership in a company and typically come with voting rights at shareholder meetings. Investors in common stocks have the potential to receive dividends and benefit from capital appreciation. Preferred stocks, on the other hand, offer fixed dividends but usually do not come with voting rights. Understanding the characteristics, benefits, and risks associated with each type of stock is crucial for making informed investment decisions.

C. Performing Research and Analysis Before Investing
Successful stock market investing requires thorough research and analysis before making investment decisions. Before investing in a particular stock, take the time to research the company's financial health, business model, competitive position, growth prospects, and management team. Key sources of information for conducting research include company annual reports, financial statements, earnings reports, analyst research reports, and news articles. Additionally, utilize fundamental analysis techniques such as analyzing financial ratios, cash flow analysis, and qualitative factors to assess the intrinsic value and growth potential of a stock. By conducting comprehensive research and analysis, investors can make informed investment decisions based on sound fundamentals and objective criteria.

As you embark on your journey into stock market investing, remember that knowledge and preparation are key. By opening a brokerage account, understanding different types of stocks, and performing thorough research and analysis, you lay the foundation for successful investing in the stock market. In the chapters that follow, we will delve deeper into the principles, strategies, and techniques for building and managing a profitable stock portfolio.

Chapter 3

II: Fundamental Analysis: Evaluating Stocks

In this chapter, we delve into the essential principles of fundamental analysis, equipping you with the knowledge and tools to evaluate stocks based on their underlying financial performance, competitive position, and growth prospects.

A. Understanding Financial Statements

To effectively evaluate stocks, it's crucial to understand the three primary financial statements: the income statement, the balance sheet, and the cash flow statement. The income statement provides a snapshot of a company's revenues, expenses, and profitability over a specific period, revealing its ability to generate profits. The balance sheet offers insights into a company's assets, liabilities, and shareholders' equity at a given point in time, providing a snapshot of its financial health and solvency. The cash flow statement tracks the flow of cash in and out of a company, highlighting its ability to generate cash and manage liquidity. By analyzing these financial statements in conjunction, investors can gain a comprehensive understanding of a company's financial performance and stability.

B. Analyzing Key Financial Ratios

Key financial ratios serve as valuable tools for assessing a company's financial health and performance relative to its peers and industry benchmarks. Commonly used financial ratios include the price-to-earnings (P/E) ratio, which compares a company's stock price to its earnings per share (EPS) and provides insights into its valuation relative to its earnings. The debt-to-equity ratio measures a company's leverage by comparing its debt to its shareholders' equity, indicating its ability to repay debt obligations. Other important ratios include the return on equity (ROE), earnings growth rate, and dividend yield, among others. By analyzing these financial ratios, investors can gauge a company's profitability, financial leverage, efficiency, and growth potential, informing their investment decisions accordingly.

C. Assessing a Company's Competitive Position and Growth Prospects

In addition to analyzing financial statements and ratios, it's essential to assess a company's competitive position and growth prospects within its industry and market environment. Factors to consider include the company's market share, competitive advantages (such as patents, brand recognition, or proprietary technology), industry trends and dynamics, customer base, and product or service innovation. By evaluating these qualitative factors alongside quantitative metrics, investors can gain a holistic understanding of a company's competitive strength and growth potential. Furthermore, conducting industry and market research, monitoring macroeconomic trends, and staying abreast of regulatory developments can provide valuable insights into a company's future prospects and investment outlook.

By mastering the principles of fundamental analysis - understanding financial statements, analyzing key financial ratios, and assessing a company's competitive position and growth prospects—you empower yourself to make informed investment decisions based on thorough research and objective analysis. In the chapters that follow, we will delve deeper into the strategies and techniques for applying fundamental analysis to identify high-quality stocks and build a profitable investment portfolio.

Chapter 4

IV: Technical Analysis: Reading Stock Charts

In this chapter, we delve into the fundamentals of technical analysis, a powerful tool for analyzing stock price movements and identifying potential trading opportunities. We'll explore the basics of technical analysis, common technical indicators, and how to use chart patterns to make informed buy and sell decisions.

A. Basics of Technical Analysis Technical analysis involves analyzing historical price and volume data to forecast future price movements. One of the fundamental concepts of technical analysis is the use of trendlines, which are lines drawn on a stock chart to connect successive highs or lows. Trendlines help identify the direction of the trend, whether it's bullish (upward) or bearish (downward). Additionally, support and resistance levels are key technical indicators that represent price levels where buying and selling pressure converge. Support levels act as floors, preventing prices from falling further, while resistance levels act as ceilings, capping price gains.

B. Common Technical Indicators Technical analysts use a variety of technical indicators to assess market trends and momentum. Moving averages are one of the most widely used indicators, which smooth out price fluctuations and provide insights into the direction of the trend. Another popular indicator is the relative strength index (RSI), which measures the magnitude of recent price changes to determine whether a stock is overbought or oversold. Other common technical indicators include MACD (Moving Average Convergence Divergence), stochastic oscillators, and

Bollinger Bands, each offering unique insights into market dynamics and potential trading opportunities.

C. Using Chart Patterns to Identify Buy and Sell Signals Chart patterns are visual representations of historical price movements that repeat over time and can provide valuable insights into future price direction. Common chart patterns include head and shoulders, double tops and bottoms, triangles, flags, and pennants. By recognizing these patterns and understanding their significance, technical analysts can identify potential buy and sell signals. For example, a breakout above a resistance level or a bullish reversal pattern may signal a buying opportunity, while a breakdown below support or a bearish reversal pattern may indicate a potential selling opportunity.

By mastering the basics of technical analysis, understanding common technical indicators, and learning to identify chart patterns, investors can gain valuable insights into market trends and make more informed trading decisions. While technical analysis is just one tool in the investor's toolbox, when used in conjunction with fundamental analysis and risk management strategies, it can enhance the probability of success in the stock market. In the chapters that follow, we will continue to explore advanced techniques and strategies for maximizing profits and minimizing risks in stock market investing.

Chapter 5

V: Developing an Investment Strategy

In this chapter, we delve into the crucial process of developing an investment strategy tailored to your financial goals, risk tolerance, and time horizon. By establishing clear objectives and aligning your investment strategy with your individual preferences and circumstances, you can lay the groundwork for a successful and sustainable approach to stock market investing.

A. Setting Investment Goals and Objectives Before diving into the world of stock market investing, it's essential to define your investment goals and objectives. Are you investing for retirement, wealth accumulation, education expenses, or a specific financial milestone? Clarifying your goals will help you determine the appropriate investment strategy and asset allocation to achieve them. Consider factors such as time horizon, desired rate of return, liquidity needs, and risk tolerance when setting your investment objectives.

B. Determining Asset Allocation and Diversification Asset allocation and diversification are critical components of any investment strategy, helping to manage risk and optimize returns over the long term. Asset allocation involves deciding how to distribute your investment capital across different asset classes such as stocks, bonds, cash, and real estate. Diversification entails spreading your investments within each asset class to minimize exposure to any single security or sector. By diversifying your portfolio across various asset classes and investment categories, you can reduce the impact of market volatility and enhance overall portfolio resilience.

C. Creating a Personalized Investment Strategy Based on Risk Tolerance and Time Horizon Your risk tolerance and time horizon are key determinants of your investment strategy and asset allocation decisions. Risk tolerance refers to your ability and willingness to withstand fluctuations in the value of your investments. It's important to assess your risk tolerance objectively and align your investment strategy accordingly, balancing the potential for higher returns with the capacity to tolerate market downturns. Additionally, consider your investment time horizon—the length of time you intend to hold your investments before needing to access the funds. Your time horizon will influence your asset allocation and investment choices, with longer time horizons typically allowing for more aggressive investment strategies focused on growth.

By developing a clear investment strategy rooted in your financial goals, risk tolerance, and time horizon, you can navigate the complexities of the stock market with confidence and discipline. In the chapters that follow, we will explore various investment strategies and techniques for building and managing a diversified portfolio designed to achieve your long-term financial objectives.

Chapter 6

VI: Building a Stock Portfolio

In this chapter, we delve into the process of building a robust and diversified stock portfolio, covering the selection of individual stocks, consideration of exchange-traded funds (ETFs) and mutual funds, constructing a diversified portfolio, and the importance of regular portfolio monitoring and rebalancing.

A. Selecting Individual Stocks vs. Investing in ETFs or Mutual Funds When building a stock portfolio, investors have the option to select individual stocks or invest in diversified funds such as ETFs or mutual funds. Individual stock selection offers the potential for higher returns but also carries higher risk due to the lack of diversification. On the other hand, investing in ETFs or mutual funds provides instant diversification across a basket of stocks or other assets, reducing individual stock risk while still offering exposure to the overall market or specific sectors. Consider your risk tolerance, investment goals, and time horizon when deciding between individual stocks and funds.

B. Constructing a Diversified Portfolio Across Different Sectors and Industries Diversification is a fundamental principle of portfolio construction, helping to mitigate risk by spreading investments across different asset classes, sectors, and industries. When building a stock portfolio, aim to diversify across various sectors such as technology, healthcare, consumer goods, finance, and energy, as well as different industries within each sector. By diversifying your holdings, you reduce the impact of adverse events affecting any single stock or sector, thereby enhancing portfolio stability and reducing overall risk.

C. Rebalancing and Monitoring the Portfolio Regularly Once your stock portfolio is established, it's essential to regularly monitor its performance and make adjustments as needed through portfolio rebalancing. Rebalancing involves periodically reviewing your portfolio's asset allocation and making adjustments to maintain your desired risk exposure and investment objectives. This may involve selling winners to take profits and reinvesting in underperforming assets to maintain your target asset allocation. Regular portfolio monitoring allows you to stay informed about market developments, track individual stock performance, and make informed decisions to optimize your portfolio's risk-return profile over time.

Building a stock portfolio is a dynamic and ongoing process that requires careful planning, disciplined execution, and continuous monitoring. By selecting individual stocks or diversified funds, constructing a diversified portfolio across different sectors and industries, and regularly monitoring and rebalancing your portfolio, you can build a solid foundation for long-term investment success. In the chapters that follow, we will explore advanced portfolio management strategies and techniques to further enhance your investment outcomes and achieve your financial goals.

Chapter 7

VII: Risk Management Strategies

In this chapter, we explore essential risk management strategies to safeguard your stock investments and mitigate potential losses. By implementing these strategies, you can protect your portfolio from adverse market movements and preserve your capital over the long term.

A. Setting Stop-Loss Orders to Limit Losses Stop-loss orders are a crucial tool for managing risk and protecting against significant losses in your stock investments. A stop-loss order is an instruction placed with your broker to sell a stock if its price falls below a specified level, known as the stop price. By setting stop-loss orders, you establish predefined exit points for your trades, helping to limit losses and prevent emotional decision-making during periods of market volatility. When setting stop-loss levels, consider factors such as your risk tolerance, investment objectives, and the stock's historical price volatility.

B. Hedging Strategies to Protect Against Downside Risk Hedging strategies are another effective way to manage risk and protect your portfolio from downside exposure. Hedging involves taking offsetting positions in related assets or derivatives to reduce the impact of adverse price movements in your stock investments. Common hedging techniques include purchasing put options, short selling, and using inverse exchange-traded funds (ETFs). By hedging your portfolio against downside risk, you can mitigate potential losses during market downturns and preserve your capital in volatile market conditions.

C. Position Sizing and Managing Portfolio Risk Position sizing and portfolio risk management are essential aspects of prudent investing that help ensure proper capital allocation and risk control. Position sizing involves determining the appropriate size of each investment position in your portfolio based on factors such as risk tolerance, investment objectives, and portfolio diversification. By diversifying your holdings across different asset classes, sectors, and industries, you spread risk and reduce the impact of adverse events affecting any single position. Additionally, regularly monitor and assess your portfolio's risk exposure using metrics such as beta, volatility, and maximum drawdown, and adjust your position sizes accordingly to maintain your desired risk-return profile.

By incorporating risk management strategies such as setting stop-loss orders, implementing hedging techniques, and practicing prudent position sizing and portfolio risk management, you can protect your stock investments from downside risk and preserve your capital over the long term. In the chapters that follow, we will delve deeper into advanced risk management techniques and explore additional strategies to enhance your investment outcomes and achieve your financial goals.

Chapter 8

VIII: Understanding Market Cycles and Economic Indicators

In this chapter, we explore the dynamics of market cycles and the role of economic indicators in shaping investment decisions. By understanding different stages of the economic cycle and utilizing various indicators to gauge economic health, investors can adapt their investment strategies to capitalize on opportunities and mitigate risks in changing market conditions.

A. Identifying Different Stages of the Economic Cycle
The economic cycle, also known as the business cycle, is characterized by alternating periods of expansion and contraction in economic activity. By recognizing different stages of the economic cycle, investors can anticipate trends in corporate earnings, interest rates, and consumer spending, providing valuable insights for investment decision-making. The four primary stages of the economic cycle include expansion, peak, contraction (recession), and trough. During the expansion phase, economic activity accelerates, leading to rising corporate profits and bullish market sentiment. At the peak, economic growth reaches its zenith, signaling the onset of a potential downturn. The contraction phase is characterized by declining economic activity, falling corporate earnings, and pessimistic market sentiment. Finally, the trough marks the bottom of the economic cycle, signaling the beginning of a recovery period.

B. Using Leading, Lagging, and Coincident Indicators to Gauge Economic Health Economic indicators are metrics that provide insights into the health and direction of the economy. Leading indicators, such as stock market performance, building permits, and consumer confidence, precede changes in economic activity and are used to forecast future trends. Lagging indicators, such as unemployment rate and corporate profits, follow changes in economic activity and confirm the direction of the economy. Coincident indicators, such as gross domestic product (GDP) and industrial production, move in tandem with changes in economic activity and provide real-time insights into the current state of the economy. By analyzing a combination of leading, lagging, and coincident indicators, investors can develop a comprehensive understanding of economic trends and adjust their investment strategies accordingly.

C. Adapting Investment Strategies Based on Current Market Conditions Successful investors adapt their investment strategies to prevailing market conditions, leveraging economic indicators and market analysis to identify opportunities and mitigate risks. During periods of economic expansion, investors may adopt a growth-oriented strategy, focusing on sectors and industries poised to benefit from rising consumer spending and corporate profits. Conversely, during economic contractions or recessions, investors may adopt a defensive strategy, emphasizing asset preservation and income generation through defensive sectors such as utilities and consumer staples. By remaining flexible and responsive to changing market conditions, investors can navigate market cycles with confidence and optimize their investment outcomes over the long term.

By understanding market cycles, utilizing economic indicators, and adapting investment strategies based on current market conditions, investors can make informed decisions and position themselves for success in the dynamic world of stock market investing. In the chapters that follow, we will delve deeper into advanced strategies and techniques to further enhance your investment skills and achieve your financial goals.

Chapter 9

IX: Psychology of Investing: Emotions and Decision-Making

In this chapter, we explore the profound impact of human psychology on investment decisions and strategies. By understanding the common biases, managing emotions, and cultivating a rational mindset, investors can make more informed and successful investment choices.

A. Common Biases and Cognitive Errors that Influence Investment Decisions Investment decisions are often influenced by cognitive biases and psychological factors that can lead to irrational behavior and suboptimal outcomes. Common biases include confirmation bias, where investors seek information that confirms their pre-existing beliefs, and anchoring bias, where investors rely too heavily on initial information when making decisions. Other biases include herd mentality, overconfidence, and loss aversion, all of which can distort judgment and lead to investment mistakes. By recognizing and mitigating these biases, investors can make more rational and objective decisions.

B. Managing Emotions Such as Fear, Greed, and Overconfidence Emotions play a significant role in investment decision-making, often leading to impulsive actions and irrational behavior. Fear and greed, in particular, can drive investors to make emotionally charged decisions based on short-term market fluctuations rather than long-term fundamentals. Similarly, overconfidence can lead investors to overestimate their abilities and take excessive risks. By cultivating self-awareness and emotional intelligence, investors can better manage their emotions and avoid succumbing to fear, greed, or overconfidence.

Techniques such as mindfulness, meditation, and cognitive behavioral therapy can help investors develop emotional resilience and maintain a disciplined approach to investing.

C. Developing a Rational and Disciplined Mindset for Successful Investing Successful investing requires a rational and disciplined mindset that prioritizes long-term goals over short-term emotions. By focusing on fundamental analysis, objective research, and prudent risk management, investors can make informed decisions based on facts and data rather than emotions or impulses. Developing a disciplined investment plan and sticking to it, even during periods of market volatility or uncertainty, is essential for long-term success. Additionally, maintaining a rational mindset requires continuous learning, adaptation, and self-reflection to identify and address any cognitive biases or emotional triggers that may arise.

By understanding the psychology of investing, managing emotions, and cultivating a rational mindset, investors can enhance their decision-making processes and achieve greater success in the stock market. In the chapters that follow, we will explore practical strategies and techniques for applying these principles to real-world investment scenarios, empowering investors to navigate the complexities of the market with confidence and clarity.

Chapter 10

X: Growth Investing: Finding High-Potential Stocks

In this chapter, we delve into the exciting realm of growth investing, where investors seek out high-potential stocks with the capacity for significant earnings and revenue growth. By identifying emerging opportunities, screening for promising growth stocks, and assessing management quality and innovation potential, investors can position themselves to capitalize on the growth potential of dynamic companies.

A. Identifying Growth Opportunities in Emerging Industries and Sectors Growth investing begins with identifying emerging industries and sectors that exhibit strong growth potential due to technological advancements, changing consumer preferences, or regulatory shifts. By staying abreast of market trends, conducting thorough industry research, and monitoring macroeconomic indicators, investors can pinpoint promising growth opportunities before they fully materialize. Whether it's renewable energy, artificial intelligence, biotechnology, or e-commerce, identifying nascent industries poised for rapid expansion is key to growth investing success.

B. Screening for Growth Stocks with Strong Earnings Growth and Revenue Growth Once potential growth opportunities have been identified, investors can employ screening techniques to filter for stocks with strong earnings growth and revenue growth prospects. Key metrics to consider include earnings per share (EPS) growth rates, revenue growth rates, and profit margins. Additionally, factors such as competitive positioning, market share, and product differentiation can provide insights into a company's growth trajectory. By focusing on companies with a track record of consistent growth and a clear path to future expansion, investors can build a portfolio poised for long-term success.

C. Assessing Management Quality and Innovation Potential In addition to financial metrics, assessing management quality and innovation potential is critical when evaluating growth stocks. A strong management team with a proven track record of execution and strategic vision can drive innovation, capitalize on market opportunities, and navigate challenges effectively. Investors should also evaluate a company's research and development (R&D) efforts, intellectual property portfolio, and commitment to innovation to gauge its potential for sustainable growth. By investing in companies with visionary leadership and a culture of innovation, investors can position themselves to benefit from disruptive technologies and market-leading products and services.

By identifying growth opportunities in emerging industries, screening for promising growth stocks, and assessing management quality and innovation potential, investors can build a growth-focused portfolio poised for long-term success. In the chapters that follow, we will explore advanced strategies and techniques for growth investing, empowering investors to uncover high-potential stocks and achieve superior investment returns in the dynamic world of the stock market.

Chapter 11

XI: Value Investing: Uncovering Undervalued Stocks

In this chapter, we delve into the principles and strategies of value investing, a time-tested approach that focuses on identifying undervalued stocks trading below their intrinsic value. By understanding the core principles of value investing, utilizing fundamental analysis techniques, and employing strategies to buy low and sell high, investors can uncover hidden gems in the stock market and achieve superior returns over the long term.

A. Principles of Value Investing and the Margin of Safety Concept Value investing is grounded in the principle of buying stocks trading at a discount to their intrinsic value, thereby providing a margin of safety for investors. The margin of safety concept, popularized by legendary investor Benjamin Graham, emphasizes the importance of purchasing stocks at prices significantly below their intrinsic value to protect against downside risk. By focusing on companies with strong fundamentals, stable earnings, and sound balance sheets, value investors seek to minimize the risk of permanent capital loss while maximizing potential upside returns over time.

B. Using Fundamental Analysis to Identify Undervalued Stocks Fundamental analysis lies at the heart of value investing, enabling investors to assess the intrinsic value of a stock based on its underlying business fundamentals. Key metrics such as price-to-earnings (P/E) ratio, price-to-book (P/B) ratio, and dividend yield are used to evaluate a company's valuation relative to its earnings, book value, and dividend payouts. Additionally, qualitative factors such as competitive positioning, brand strength, and management quality play a crucial role in determining a company's intrinsic value. By conducting thorough fundamental analysis, value investors can identify undervalued stocks trading at a discount to their true worth.

C. Strategies for Buying Low and Selling High in Value Investing Value investing is not just about identifying undervalued stocks but also about timing your purchases and sales to maximize returns. One strategy employed by value investors is to accumulate stocks when they are trading below their intrinsic value, taking advantage of market inefficiencies and temporary downturns to build positions at attractive prices. Conversely, value investors may sell stocks when they become overvalued or when the market price exceeds the company's intrinsic value, thereby locking in profits and reallocating capital to more undervalued opportunities. By adhering to a disciplined approach of buying low and selling high, value investors can capitalize on market mispricings and generate superior investment returns over the long term.

By embracing the principles of value investing, utilizing fundamental analysis techniques, and employing strategies to buy low and sell high, investors can uncover undervalued stocks and build a portfolio poised for long-term success. In the chapters that follow, we will explore advanced value investing strategies and techniques to further enhance your investment outcomes and achieve your financial goals.

Chapter 12

XII: Sector and Industry Analysis

In this chapter, we explore the importance of sector and industry analysis in stock market investing, focusing on understanding sector rotation, analyzing competitive landscapes, and identifying opportunities and risks within specific sectors for strategic investment decisions.

A. Understanding Sector Rotation and Industry Trends
Sector rotation refers to the cyclical movement of investor capital among different sectors of the economy based on changing market conditions, economic trends, and investor sentiment. By understanding sector rotation patterns and industry trends, investors can anticipate shifts in market leadership and position their portfolios accordingly. Factors such as changes in interest rates, economic indicators, technological advancements, and regulatory policies can influence sector rotation and industry performance. By staying abreast of sector rotation dynamics and industry trends, investors can capitalize on emerging opportunities and avoid sectors poised for underperformance.

B. Analyzing the Competitive Landscape and Market
Dynamics within Specific Sectors Effective sector and industry analysis require a deep understanding of the competitive landscape and market dynamics within specific sectors. Factors such as market share, pricing power, barriers to entry, and regulatory environment can impact the competitive positioning of companies within a sector. Analyzing key industry players, their strengths and weaknesses, and strategic initiatives can provide insights into sector dynamics and competitive forces at play. By conducting comprehensive industry research and

competitive analysis, investors can identify sector leaders, disruptors, and laggards, enabling informed investment decisions.

C. Identifying Opportunities and Risks in Different Sectors for Strategic Investment Decisions Sector and industry analysis help investors identify opportunities and risks within different sectors for strategic investment decisions. Some sectors may offer attractive growth prospects due to favorable industry trends, technological innovations, or demographic shifts, while others may face headwinds such as regulatory challenges, competitive pressures, or changing consumer preferences. By assessing opportunities and risks within various sectors, investors can allocate capital strategically, overweighting sectors with strong growth potential and underweighting sectors facing challenges or headwinds. Additionally, sector analysis can inform sector rotation strategies, allowing investors to capitalize on market cycles and shifting investor preferences.

By understanding sector rotation, analyzing competitive landscapes, and identifying opportunities and risks within specific sectors, investors can make informed investment decisions and build portfolios poised for long-term success. In the chapters that follow, we will explore advanced sector and industry analysis techniques and strategies to further enhance your investment outcomes and achieve your financial goals.

Chapter 13

XIII: Trading Strategies and Techniques

In this chapter, we explore various trading strategies and techniques that investors can employ to profit from the dynamic movements of the stock market. Whether you're interested in day trading, swing trading, or long-term investing, understanding different trading styles and developing a disciplined trading plan is essential for success.

A. Day Trading vs. Swing Trading vs. Long-Term Investing Day trading involves buying and selling stocks within the same trading day, aiming to profit from short-term price fluctuations. Swing trading, on the other hand, involves holding positions for a few days to several weeks, capitalizing on intermediate-term price trends. Long-term investing focuses on buying and holding stocks for the long term, with the goal of maximizing returns over an extended period. Each trading style has its advantages and challenges, and investors should choose a strategy that aligns with their risk tolerance, time horizon, and trading objectives.

B. Momentum Trading, Trend Following, and Contrarian Strategies Momentum trading involves capitalizing on the momentum of stocks that are moving in a particular direction, either upward (uptrend) or downward (downtrend). Trend following strategies aim to ride established trends and profit from sustained price movements, while contrarian strategies seek to capitalize on reversals or countertrends in the market. By understanding market dynamics and identifying momentum shifts, trend followers and contrarian traders can anticipate price movements and position themselves for profitable trades.

C. Developing a Trading Plan and Disciplined Approach to Trading Regardless of the trading style or strategy employed, developing a trading plan and maintaining a disciplined approach to trading is crucial for success. A trading plan outlines specific criteria for entering and exiting trades, risk management rules, and profit targets. It also includes guidelines for position sizing, trade execution, and trade monitoring. By adhering to a well-defined trading plan and exercising discipline in executing trades, traders can minimize emotional decision-making, reduce impulsive behavior, and improve consistency in trading performance.

Incorporating trading strategies such as day trading, swing trading, or long-term investing, along with techniques like momentum trading, trend following, and contrarian strategies, can enhance your ability to profit from the stock market's dynamic movements. By developing a trading plan and maintaining discipline in your trading approach, you can navigate the complexities of the market with confidence and achieve your financial goals. In the chapters that follow, we will explore advanced trading strategies and techniques to further enhance your trading skills and optimize your investment outcomes.

Chapter 14

XIV: Psychology of Investing: Emotions and Decision-Making

In this chapter, we delve deeper into the psychology of investing, exploring the profound impact of human emotions and cognitive biases on investment decisions. By understanding common biases, managing emotions effectively, and cultivating a rational mindset, investors can make more informed and successful investment choices.

A. Common Biases and Cognitive Errors that Influence Investment Decisions Investment decisions are often influenced by cognitive biases and psychological factors that can lead to irrational behavior and suboptimal outcomes. Common biases include confirmation bias, where investors seek information that confirms their pre-existing beliefs, and anchoring bias, where investors rely too heavily on initial information when making decisions. Other biases include herd mentality, overconfidence, and loss aversion, all of which can distort judgment and lead to investment mistakes. By recognizing and mitigating these biases, investors can make more rational and objective decisions.

B. Managing Emotions Such as Fear, Greed, and Overconfidence Emotions play a significant role in investment decision-making, often leading to impulsive actions and irrational behavior. Fear and greed, in particular, can drive investors to make emotionally charged decisions based on short-term market fluctuations rather than long-term fundamentals. Similarly, overconfidence can lead investors to overestimate their abilities and take excessive risks. By cultivating self-awareness and emotional intelligence, investors can better manage their emotions and avoid succumbing to fear, greed, or overconfidence. Techniques such as mindfulness, meditation, and cognitive behavioral therapy can help investors develop emotional resilience and maintain a disciplined approach to investing.

C. Developing a Rational and Disciplined Mindset for Successful Investing Successful investing requires a rational and disciplined mindset that prioritizes long-term goals over short-term emotions. By focusing on fundamental analysis, objective research, and prudent risk management, investors can make informed decisions based on facts and data rather than emotions or impulses. Developing a disciplined investment plan and sticking to it, even during periods of market volatility or uncertainty, is essential for long-term success. Additionally, maintaining a rational mindset requires continuous learning, adaptation, and self-reflection to identify and address any cognitive biases or emotional triggers that may arise.

By understanding the psychology of investing, managing emotions, and cultivating a rational mindset, investors can enhance their decision-making processes and achieve greater success in the stock market. In the chapters that follow, we will explore practical strategies and techniques for applying these principles to real-world investment scenarios, empowering investors to navigate the complexities of the market with confidence and clarity.

Chapter 15

XV: Tax Strategies and Considerations

In this chapter, we delve into the essential tax strategies and considerations for stock market investors. Understanding the tax implications of your investment decisions, utilizing tax-advantaged accounts, and implementing tax-efficient strategies can help minimize your tax liabilities and maximize your after-tax returns.

A. Understanding the Tax Implications of Stock Market Investing Stock market investing can have significant tax implications, impacting both your investment returns and overall tax liabilities. Key tax considerations include capital gains taxes on profits realized from selling stocks, dividend taxes on income received from dividend-paying stocks, and potential taxes on interest income or other investment gains. Additionally, different types of accounts, such as taxable brokerage accounts, retirement accounts, and tax-advantaged accounts, may have varying tax treatments. By understanding the tax consequences of your investment decisions, you can make informed choices to optimize your after-tax returns.

B. Utilizing Tax-Advantaged Accounts such as IRAs and 401(k)s Tax-advantaged retirement accounts, such as Individual Retirement Accounts (IRAs) and 401(k) plans, offer valuable tax benefits that can help investors grow their investments more efficiently. Contributions to traditional IRAs and 401(k) plans are typically tax-deductible, reducing your current taxable income and allowing your investments to grow tax-deferred until retirement. Roth IRAs and Roth 401(k) plans, on the other hand, offer tax-free withdrawals in retirement, providing valuable tax diversification and flexibility. By maximizing contributions to tax-advantaged accounts and taking advantage of employer-sponsored retirement plans, investors can optimize their long-term wealth accumulation and minimize their tax burdens.

C. Implementing Tax-Loss Harvesting and Other Tax-Efficient Strategies Tax-loss harvesting is a tax-efficient strategy that involves selling investments at a loss to offset capital gains and reduce taxable income. By strategically realizing losses, investors can reduce their tax liabilities while maintaining exposure to the market and potentially enhancing after-tax returns. Other tax-efficient strategies include asset location, which involves holding tax-efficient investments in taxable accounts and tax-inefficient investments in tax-advantaged accounts, and avoiding short-term capital gains by holding investments for more than one year to qualify for lower long-term capital gains tax rates. By implementing these tax-efficient strategies, investors can enhance their after-tax returns and minimize the impact of taxes on their investment portfolios.

By understanding the tax implications of stock market investing, utilizing tax-advantaged accounts, and implementing tax-efficient strategies such as tax-loss harvesting, investors can minimize their tax liabilities and maximize their after-tax returns. In the chapters that follow, we will explore advanced tax planning techniques and strategies to further optimize your investment outcomes and achieve your financial goals.

Chapter 16

XVI: Advanced Trading Techniques and Tools

In this chapter, we explore advanced trading techniques and tools that sophisticated traders use to gain a competitive edge in the stock market. From leveraged trading strategies to algorithmic trading systems and advanced technical analysis tools, mastering these techniques can enhance your trading performance and maximize your profits.

A. Leveraged Trading Strategies (e.g., Options, Futures, Margin Trading) Leveraged trading strategies involve using borrowed funds or financial derivatives such as options and futures to amplify returns and gain exposure to the market beyond your initial investment. Options allow traders to control a larger position with a smaller upfront investment, offering potential for significant returns while limiting downside risk. Futures contracts enable traders to speculate on the future price movements of underlying assets, such as commodities, currencies, or stock indices, with the potential for high leverage and rapid gains or losses. Margin trading involves borrowing funds from a broker to purchase securities, increasing buying power and potential returns but also amplifying losses. By understanding the risks and rewards of leveraged trading strategies, traders can capitalize on market opportunities while managing risk effectively.

B. Algorithmic Trading and Automated Trading Systems Algorithmic trading, also known as algo trading or automated trading, involves using computer algorithms to execute trading strategies automatically based on predefined rules and parameters. These algorithms analyze market data, identify trading opportunities, and execute trades at high speeds, leveraging technology to capitalize on fleeting market inefficiencies. Automated trading systems allow traders to remove human emotions and biases from the trading process, ensuring consistency and discipline in executing trades. By harnessing the power of algorithmic trading, traders can access markets 24/7, react quickly to changing market conditions, and capitalize on short-term trading opportunities with precision and efficiency.

C. Utilizing Advanced Technical Analysis Tools and Software for Trading Advanced technical analysis tools and software provide traders with powerful capabilities to analyze market data, identify patterns, and make informed trading decisions. These tools include advanced charting software, indicators, and trading platforms that offer customizable features and real-time market data. Technical analysis tools such as moving averages, Bollinger Bands, and Fibonacci retracements help traders identify trends, support and resistance levels, and potential entry and exit points. Additionally, advanced charting techniques such as candlestick patterns, volume analysis, and chart overlays provide valuable insights into market sentiment and price action. By utilizing advanced technical analysis tools and software, traders can enhance their trading strategies, improve decision-making, and achieve better trading results.

By mastering advanced trading techniques such as leveraged trading strategies, algorithmic trading, and utilizing advanced technical analysis tools and software, traders can gain a competitive edge in the stock market and achieve superior trading performance. In the chapters that follow, we will delve deeper into these advanced trading techniques and explore practical strategies for integrating them into your trading approach.

Chapter 17

XVII: International Investing and Global Markets

In this chapter, we explore the opportunities and challenges of international investing, providing insights into the benefits and risks of investing in global markets. From strategies for accessing international stocks to understanding currency risk and geopolitical factors, mastering international investing can help diversify your portfolio and capitalize on global growth opportunities.

A. Benefits and Risks of Investing in International Markets Investing in international markets offers several benefits, including access to a broader range of investment opportunities, exposure to diverse industries and sectors, and the potential for higher returns through global economic growth. Additionally, international investing can provide portfolio diversification benefits by reducing correlation with domestic markets and mitigating country-specific risks. However, investing in international markets also comes with inherent risks, including currency fluctuations, geopolitical instability, regulatory differences, and cultural nuances. By understanding the benefits and risks of international investing, investors can make informed decisions to optimize their portfolio's risk-return profile.

B. Strategies for Accessing International Stocks and Diversifying Globally There are several strategies for accessing international stocks and diversifying globally, ranging from direct stock investments to investing in international mutual funds, exchange-traded funds (ETFs), and American Depositary Receipts (ADRs). Direct stock investments allow investors to purchase shares of foreign companies listed on international stock exchanges, providing direct exposure to specific markets and industries. Alternatively, international mutual funds and ETFs offer diversified exposure to global markets, allowing investors to gain access to international stocks with lower costs and reduced risk. Additionally, ADRs enable investors to invest in foreign companies through U.S.-listed securities, providing convenience and liquidity for accessing international markets. By utilizing these strategies, investors can effectively diversify their portfolios and capitalize on global growth opportunities.

C. Understanding Currency Risk and Geopolitical Factors that Impact Global Markets Currency risk, also known as exchange rate risk, is a significant consideration for international investors, as fluctuations in currency exchange rates can impact the value of international investments denominated in foreign currencies. Geopolitical factors such as trade tensions, political instability, and regulatory changes can also affect global markets and influence investment returns. By staying informed about geopolitical developments and monitoring currency trends, investors can better navigate the complexities of international investing and manage currency risk effectively. Additionally, diversifying investments across different regions and currencies can help mitigate the impact of geopolitical events and currency fluctuations on investment portfolios.

By embracing international investing and understanding the benefits and risks of global markets, investors can diversify their portfolios, access new growth opportunities, and enhance their investment outcomes. In the chapters that follow, we will explore advanced strategies and techniques for international investing, empowering investors to navigate global markets with confidence and achieve their financial goals.

Chapter 18

XVIII: Special Situations and Investment Opportunities

In this chapter, we explore special situations and investment opportunities that arise from unique corporate events, market anomalies, and specialized sectors. By identifying special situations such as mergers and acquisitions, spin-offs, and IPOs, and implementing strategies to profit from these events, investors can capitalize on unique investment opportunities and potentially achieve superior returns.

A. Identifying Special Situations Such as Mergers and Acquisitions, Spin-offs, and IPOs Special situations refer to unique corporate events or circumstances that can create investment opportunities for astute investors. These events may include mergers and acquisitions, where companies combine or acquire other companies to achieve strategic objectives or unlock synergies. Spin-offs involve the separation of a subsidiary or division from its parent company, creating independent entities with distinct investment characteristics. Initial Public Offerings (IPOs) represent the first sale of a company's shares to the public, providing investors with an opportunity to invest in newly listed companies. By identifying and analyzing special situations, investors can uncover undervalued assets and potential catalysts for stock price appreciation.

B. Strategies for Profiting from Corporate Events and Market Anomalies Profiting from corporate events and market anomalies requires a deep understanding of market dynamics, investor psychology, and the factors driving these events. Strategies for capitalizing on special situations may include event-driven investing, where investors anticipate and position themselves ahead of corporate events such as mergers, acquisitions, or spin-offs to capture potential gains. Additionally, contrarian strategies may involve taking advantage of market mispricings or irrational investor behavior to buy undervalued assets or sell overvalued ones. By employing these strategies, investors can exploit market inefficiencies and generate alpha in their investment portfolios.

C. Navigating Unique Investment Opportunities in Distressed Assets, Turnaround Situations, and Special Sectors In addition to corporate events, investors can also explore unique investment opportunities in distressed assets, turnaround situations, and special sectors. Distressed assets may include companies facing financial distress or bankruptcy, offering potential opportunities for value-oriented investors to acquire assets at distressed prices. Turnaround situations involve investing in companies with turnaround potential, where operational improvements or strategic changes can unlock value and drive stock price appreciation. Special sectors such as renewable energy, cannabis, or technology can also present niche investment opportunities for investors with specialized knowledge or expertise. By navigating these unique investment opportunities, investors can diversify their portfolios and access potential sources of alpha in the market.

By identifying special situations, implementing strategies to profit from corporate events and market anomalies, and navigating unique investment opportunities in distressed assets, turnaround situations, and special sectors, investors can uncover hidden gems and unlock value in their investment portfolios. In the chapters that follow, we will delve deeper into these special situations and explore practical strategies for capitalizing on unique investment opportunities.

Chapter 19

XIX: Socially Responsible Investing (SRI) and ESG Investing

In this chapter, we explore the principles of socially responsible investing (SRI) and environmental, social, and governance (ESG) criteria, providing insights into how investors can align their investment decisions with their values while achieving financial returns. From screening for sustainable and ethical investments to balancing financial returns with social and environmental impact considerations, socially responsible investing offers investors an opportunity to make a positive difference in the world while growing their wealth.

A. Principles of Socially Responsible Investing and Environmental, Social, and Governance (ESG) Criteria
Socially responsible investing (SRI) and environmental, social, and governance (ESG) investing focus on integrating environmental, social, and governance factors into investment decisions, alongside financial considerations. ESG criteria encompass a broad range of factors, including environmental sustainability, social responsibility, and corporate governance practices. Investors may prioritize companies with strong ESG performance, transparent corporate governance, and a commitment to ethical business practices. By aligning their investments with their values, investors can support companies that promote sustainability, social justice, and responsible corporate behavior.

B. Screening for Sustainable and Ethical Investments
Screening for sustainable and ethical investments involves evaluating companies based on ESG criteria and excluding those that engage in controversial or harmful practices.

Positive screening identifies companies that demonstrate strong ESG performance and align with investors' values, while negative screening excludes companies involved in activities such as fossil fuels, tobacco, or human rights violations. Additionally, thematic investing focuses on specific ESG themes, such as renewable energy, clean technology, or diversity and inclusion, allowing investors to support causes they believe in while generating financial returns. By screening for sustainable and ethical investments, investors can build portfolios that reflect their values and contribute to positive social and environmental outcomes.

C. Balancing Financial Returns with Social and Environmental Impact Considerations Balancing financial returns with social and environmental impact considerations is a key challenge for socially responsible investors. While SRI and ESG investing prioritize non-financial factors, investors must also consider the financial implications of their investment decisions. Studies have shown that companies with strong ESG performance tend to outperform their peers over the long term, suggesting that there may be a positive correlation between ESG factors and financial returns. However, investors must weigh the potential trade-offs between financial returns and social or environmental impact when making investment decisions. By integrating ESG considerations into their investment process and evaluating companies based on both financial and non-financial criteria, investors can strive to achieve competitive returns while making a positive difference in the world.

By embracing the principles of socially responsible investing (SRI) and environmental, social, and governance

(ESG) criteria, investors can align their investment decisions with their values and contribute to positive social and environmental outcomes while achieving financial returns. In the chapters that follow, we will delve deeper into SRI and ESG investing strategies and explore practical techniques for integrating these principles into your investment approach.

Chapter 20

XX: Conclusion and Next Steps

In this final chapter, we recap the essential lessons and insights covered in this book and provide guidance on how to continue your journey toward becoming a successful stock market investor. We'll review key takeaways, offer encouragement for ongoing learning and growth, and provide resources for further education and development.

A. Reviewing Key Takeaways and Actionable Insights from the Book Throughout this book, you've learned about various aspects of stock market investing, from understanding the fundamentals of investing and analyzing stocks to implementing advanced trading strategies and exploring unique investment opportunities. You've gained insights into the importance of portfolio diversification, risk management, and discipline in investing. You've also explored different investment styles and approaches, from value investing and growth investing to socially responsible investing and global markets. By reviewing and reflecting on the key takeaways and actionable insights from each chapter, you can reinforce your understanding and apply these principles to your investment journey.

B. Encouragement for Continued Learning and Growth as an Investor Investing is a lifelong journey, and there's always more to learn and explore. As you continue your investment journey, embrace a growth mindset and remain open to new ideas and perspectives. Seek out opportunities for ongoing learning and education, whether through reading books, attending seminars, or participating in online courses. Surround yourself with experienced investors, mentors, and peers who can provide guidance and support along the way.

Remember that investing is as much about personal growth and development as it is about building wealth. Stay curious, stay disciplined, and stay committed to your long-term financial goals.

C. Resources for Further Education, Including Books, Websites, and Financial Education Programs To further enhance your investment knowledge and skills, consider exploring additional resources and educational materials. There are countless books, websites, and financial education programs available that cover a wide range of topics related to investing, finance, and personal development. Look for reputable sources of information and seek out resources that align with your interests and learning objectives. Whether you're interested in mastering technical analysis, learning about the latest investment trends, or delving into the intricacies of options trading, there's a wealth of resources available to support your continued education and development as an investor.

In conclusion, remember that investing in stocks is a journey that requires patience, discipline, and continuous learning. By applying the principles and strategies outlined in this book, you can navigate the complexities of the stock market with confidence and achieve your financial goals. Stay focused, stay informed, and stay committed to your journey toward financial success. The world of investing is vast and ever-evolving, and the opportunities for growth and prosperity are limitless. Embrace the journey, and may your investment endeavors be rewarding and fulfilling.

www.ingramcontent.com/pod-product-compliance
Lightning Source LLC
Chambersburg PA
CBHW070442290526
45791CB00005B/2069